Date Due

BRODART, CO.   Cat. No. 23-233-003   Printed in U.S.A.

Bound for America

*The Story of the
European Immigrants*

GREAT JOURNEYS

Bound for America

The Story of the European Immigrants

by Milton Meltzer

BENCHMARK BOOKS

MARSHALL CAVENDISH
NEW YORK

Benchmark Books
Marshall Cavendish Corporation
99 White Plains Road
Tarrytown, NY 10591-9001

Cover photograph: *Secondino Libro, a ten year old, poses in 1911 with other young workers at a
textile mill in Lawrence, Massachusetts.*
Photo research by Candlepants Incorporated
Cover photo: Corbis
The photographs in this book are used by permission and through the courtesy of:
Corbis, 12, 19, 22, 39, 42, 59, 78, 83, 84, 93, 97; Bettmann, 2-3, 8, 10, 14, 16, 20, 28,
49, 50, 52, 60, 64, 68, 70, 74, 75, 77, 86, 88; Austrian Archives, 45; Hulton Deutsch
Collection, 46, 90; Michael Maslin Historic Photographs, 56; James Marshall, 98; Dean
Wong, 102. *The Granger Collection*, NY: 25 (left and right), 31, 35, 40. *Milton Meltzer*: 62.
Library of Congress: 67.

Library of Congress Cataloging-in-Publication Data
Meltzer, Milton, (date)
Bound for America: the story of the European immigrants / by Milton Meltzer.
p. cm. — (Great journeys)
Includes bibliographical references and index.
ISBN 0-7614-1227-1
1. United States—Emigration and immigration—History—Juvenile
literature. 2. Immigrants—United
States—History—Juvenile literature. [1. United States—Emigration
and immigration—History. 2. Immigrants.]   I. Title. II. Great journeys (Benchmark
Books (Firm))
JV6450.M45   2001   325.73—dc21   00-051875

Printed in the United States of America

3 5 6 4 2

Contents

Also by Milton Meltzer

Brother, Can You Spare a Dime? The Great Depression, 1929–1933

Bread and Roses: The Struggle of American Labor, 1865–1915

Cheap Raw Material: How Our Youngest Workers Are Exploited and Abused

Who Cares? Millions Do: A Book about Altruism

Carl Sandburg: A Biography

Dorothea Lange: A Photographer's Life

Ten Queens: Portraits of Women of Power

Witches and Witch-Hunts: A History of Persecution

Weapons and Warfare: From the Stone Age to the Space Age

Food: How We Hunt and Gather It, How We Grow and Eat It, How We Buy and Sell It, How We Preserve and Waste It—and How Some Have Too Much and Others Too Little of It

Foreword

IF THERE'S ONE THING THAT WE ALL SHARE, IT IS THE EXPERIENCE OF migration. We all migrated here from other parts of the world to become part of a growing and ever changing nation. America is a land of many peoples, many colors, many cultures, many religious beliefs. We speak different languages; we live and behave in different ways. But we all want one thing—to be treated equally.

As migrants, we've all shared in a great human experience. Migrations are as old as humankind. All through time people have picked up from one place and moved to another out of the simple desire for a better life. Maybe the grass was better for the herds. Or there was more water, or richer soil, or more jobs, or greater freedom, or fewer wars.

That hope of making a better life elsewhere seized millions of people in Europe in the 1800s. There was a large rise in the population and

Staring across the bay at New York: the "Promised Land"

a worsening of living conditions. As the number of people grew faster than the ability to provide food and work for them, a great many people were worse off than before. They began to think of leaving home.

To go where? And how? And what might happen when they got there? How would they live in a strange place, among new people?

This book is the story of that great migration out of Europe to America. (Other books in the Great Journeys series will tell the story of immigration from other parts of the world.) I write out of the experience of my own immigrant history. For my grandparents and my father and mother were immigrants from Europe. Of course their experience was not exactly the same as all others. But despite some important differences, there is a common core. What happened to them helps me to understand what happened to other Europeans.

Migrants packed aboard the steamship S. S. Prince Frederick Wilhelm, *entering New York harbor in 1915*

One

Three Waves

IMAGINE THE AMERICAN CONTINENT BEFORE THERE WERE ANY PEOPLE living here. A land mass of 9,400,000 square miles, it was the third largest continent on the planet Earth. Maybe 40,000 years ago the first migrants entered. It is believed they walked across a land bridge from Siberia to Alaska, an isthmus later broken by the Bering Strait.

From Alaska these ancestors of the Native Americans spread through what we now call North, Central, and South America. The first Americans lived by hunting and gathering, and then by herding and farming. Eventually they developed complex cultures in several parts of the Western Hemisphere.

Later came other migrants, small numbers of Norsemen sailing out of Iceland and Greenland around A.D. 1010. They were the first Europeans to reach America. Nearly five hundred years later, in 1492, Christopher Columbus at the head of his tiny fleet of three ships arrived,

11

In this cartoon from the nineteenth-century magazine Puck, *Uncle Sam welcomes European migrants to the "U.S. Ark of Refuge."*

and with him began a steady trickle of migrants to America. Not until after 1815 would that trickle become a flood.

Across the span of American history three waves of migration can be counted. The first wave was from the colonial time of 1600 to about 1800, when the War of Independence from Britain had been won and the new republic was established. That migration included the forced movement of Africans, enslaved in their homelands and shipped across the Atlantic to be sold for unpaid labor in the Americas. The others entering America were voluntary migrants, white, largely English and Welsh, Scotch-Irish, and German. They were mainly Protestant.

Figures for the first era are not precise. But by the time of the first census of 1790, nearly one million African Americans and four million Europeans lived in the new United States.

The second era, from about the 1820s to the 1920s (when restrictive laws were adopted), was more diverse. It included Catholics and Jews, and Southern and Eastern Europeans. Behind it was the breakdown of the traditional agricultural system in Europe and a transportation revolution, brought about by the development of steam power, which made the United States easier to reach. About 30 million people moved to America in this great wave.

The third era is the one we are in now. It began in the late 1960s, when immigration laws became more liberal, and continues to this day. The migrants are mostly Asian and Hispanic, moved to leave their homelands by bad social and economic conditions, which made refugees of many millions.

It is the second era, called the First Great Migration, that this book deals with. But before narrowing the focus, let's look at migration itself, at any time. For migration has been a force in world history for thousands of years. Why does it happen? One reason is warfare. People flee before the victors to avoid devastation and death. Others, such as Africans, migrated not voluntarily but in bondage. Beginning in the fifteenth century, they were shipped like human merchandise to wherever slave dealers wanted them to go. Sometimes people who thought themselves free have been forced to move by ruthless tyrants. The communist dictator Joseph Stalin uprooted whole ethnic populations and made them move from their home regions in the Soviet Union to remote parts of his vast empire. Then there have always been people who move because they believe some other place offers a better life.

In the Balkans and in certain African countries in the late twentieth century, "ethnic cleansing" took place, when "undesirable" people were killed or forced to move, to make room for more "politically reliable" people. So people moving willingly and peacefully is just one of the ways

A young woman from Albania at Ellis Island, as captured by Lewis Hine, a master of documentary photography

in which the populations of the world have been redistributed over the centuries.

Migration is a story with many angles. It's about the people who migrate and the place they migrate from. And it's about the land they go to and their impact there. What do the migrants take with them? What skills and beliefs and attitudes? What do they find when they cross borders into a foreign land? And how do they help shape their new home?

Migrations may be seasonal or permanent, local or global. The people who move differ considerably in how they contribute to the societies they enter. Some farm, some labor in factories or mines, some are engineers who reshape whole industries, some are scientists who build bombs or cure diseases. And some are artists who shape a personal vision of the new world they experience.

But what were the people of the 1800s like in the old country? Which of them chose to migrate, and why?

An old woman loaded with all she can carry looks to an uncertain future in her newly adopted land.

Two

The Rhythm of Migration

IT'S NOT COMMONLY REALIZED THAT FAR MORE PEOPLE MIGRATED *WITHIN* their own countries in Europe than across the Atlantic. One to two million people a year moved inside their own countries, from one farming area to another, or to nearby cities. Those who moved were usually young and unmarried, both men and women.

The total number of Europeans who migrated *outside* of Europe is hard to pin down. One estimate holds that between 1800 and 1914 about 50 million moved, three out of five going to the United States. The United States received more migrants than probably the entire world combined. (For the breakdown by country see the table on page 19.)

The rhythm of migration depends on a complex equation. It may involve changes in climate, food supply, population growth, local rivalries, distant crises. It is a delicate balance. There is the *push* of local pressures and the *pull* of happier prospects beyond the horizon. The forces of push may be catastrophic, such as the Irish potato famines of the 1840s. Or political, such as the failure of the revolutions of 1848 in Europe. Most often, they are economic pressures, such as a growing population and lack of work. The attractive forces of pull may include promises of jobs, or political or religious freedom, or a more benign climate, or freedom from military service.

As important as push and pull is the question of *means*. That is, the ability to migrate. Can you afford the cost of transportation? Does your country prohibit travel abroad? And what about the country you wish to migrate to? Does it welcome newcomers or does it put up barriers to keep them out?

Although millions migrate, the fact is that only a minority of any population is likely to pick up and leave—even under catastrophic conditions. The kinds of people who choose to leave are determined mostly by the conditions in that country. On the other hand, when conditions at home are not intolerable, still, people will leave. Why? Simply because they want to, because what they've heard about other places is very appealing, and because their skills seem right for the place they hope to settle in. But those who go because of the force of push, like people whose homeland is torn apart by war, would never have gone if it weren't for the bloody chaos.

Studies of migration movements show that people tend to leave at certain stages of life. Most often it's the young who go first. About 40 percent of Irish immigrants in the late nineteenth and early twentieth centuries were between the ages of 20 and 24. In that same period large numbers of immigrants from Greece and Italy were even younger—child laborers. In today's world many immigrants from less developed countries are recent graduates of colleges and professional schools.

Families often are unable to migrate together. The members come one at a time, helped by those who've gone before. This is called *chain migration*.

FOREIGN-BORN POPULATION IN THE UNITED STATES: 1870–1920					
	1870	**1880**	**1890**	**1900**	**1910**	**1920**
Germany	1,691,000	1,967,000	2,785,000	2,663,000	2,311,000	1,686,000
Ireland	1,856,000	1,855,000	1,872,000	1,615,000	1,352,000	1,037,000
Italy	17,000	44,000	183,000	484,000	1,343,000	1,610,000
Russia	5,000	36,000	183,000	424,000	1,184,000	1,400,000
Poland	14,000	49,000	147,000	383,000	938,000	1,140,000
England & Wales	630,000	747,000	1,009,000	934,000	960,000	881,000
Sweden	97,000	194,000	478,000	582,000	665,000	626,000
Austria	71,000	124,000	241,000	433,000	846,000	576,000
Hungary	4,000	12,000	62,000	146,000	496,000	397,000
Norway	114,000	182,000	323,000	336,000	404,000	364,000
Scotland	141,000	170,000	242,000	234,000	261,000	255,000
Denmark & Iceland	30,000	64,000	133,000	154,000	182,000	189,000
Greece	400	800	2,000	9,000	101,000	176,000
France	116,000	107,000	113,000	104,000	117,000	153,000
Switzerland	75,000	89,000	104,000	116,000	125,000	119,000
Portugal	9,000	16,000	22,000	38,000	77,000	104,000
Spain	4,000	5,000	6,000	7,000	22,000	50,000

U.S. Bureau of the Census, *Historical Statistics of the United States, Colonial Times to 1970* (Washington: Government Printing Office, 1975), series C230-C264, 1:117.

In the nineteenth century most migrants were not the poorest, not the worst-off people in their countries of origin. The people at the lowest level had neither the money nor the energy to leave, and those at the top were doing fine where they were.

Some ethnic groups, such as these Italians from Genoa, photographed onboard their ship,
traveled together to America.

What about the places within the United States that migrants chose to go to? It appears that migration moved in specific paths. It was often from a particular region, city, or village in the homeland to a specific region, city, or even neighborhood or block in America. "Stream migration" they call it. For instance, several thousand Italians from one town in Italy, Valledolmo, settled in and around Dunkirk, New York, in the late nineteenth and early twentieth centuries.

One often ignored fact about migration is that many migrants returned home. This is called the *counterstream*. Sometimes they went back for good, never returning to America. Others returned home, changed their minds, and went back to America. Some did that more than once.

But let's turn to the earliest migrants from Europe. . . .

An artist's rendering of the three ships arriving at Jamestown on May 24, 1609 to settle the Virginia colony. Within seven months, famine and disease cut their number from 105 to 32.

Three

In Colonial Times

DURING THE COLONIAL PERIOD (1607 TO ADOPTION OF THE CONSTITU-tion in 1787), fewer than a million people migrated to America. Maybe 600,000 Europeans and 300,000 Africans. (All the Africans were enslaved, and about half the Europeans, as indentured servants, were to a degree unfree.) Those colonial newcomers were scarcely 2 percent of all those who have ever come, yet they had a profound effect upon American history. Most of the Europeans spoke English, so the American language and culture became an outgrowth of British culture.

Yet at first the English settlers in America did not thrive. Those who came to Virginia were the victims of deceitful propaganda that painted the colony as a land of milk and honey. Recent studies show that the majority who crossed the Atlantic were male, young, single, poor, and ignorant. (Far more people in that era migrated *within* England, moving to and between towns, especially to London.) Those who came to

America were often indentured servants, committed to labor for a planter or a company for four to seven years. Add about 50,000 convicts England shipped off to America. (After the American Revolution, England dumped convicts on Australia.)

Hunger and sickness took the lives of many migrants in the first decades of settlement. Later, when the tobacco trade offered the promise of high profits, middle- and upper-class people came to fill the ranks of the Virginia planters. They enjoyed the good life, sweated out of the unpaid labor of slaves.

In contrast to the settlers in the South, New England's immigrants came with agricultural and craft skills, often in family groups. Many of their leaders were highly educated. Contrary to popular belief, only a minority were Pilgrims and Puritans. Most were not religious refugees but actively recruited by promoters who lured them with the promise of a better life in America. If they had owned land in England, they expected to acquire even more in America. Farm laborers hoped to become independent farmers, and servants aspired to a better status in the New World.

To get here, migrants had to find a ship. Not easy to do, for in colonial times there were no sailings on an established schedule. Groups of migrants had to find a captain and arrange for a crossing. Fares were quite costly. The ships were tiny, only forty to eighty feet long and terribly crowded. It took eight to twelve weeks to cross the Atlantic. Seasickness was common, as were scurvy and dysentery. There were few shipwrecks, however. Still, the fear of a long and perhaps dangerous voyage scared off many.

By 1700 the great majority of New Englanders were at least second-generation Americans. When the eighteenth century brought on even heavier immigration, they became increasingly cold to the arrival of "outsiders." The two largest groups entering were the Irish and the Germans.

The Catholic Irish settled throughout the colonies, while the Germans, almost all Protestants, went mostly to Pennsylvania. Benjamin

An immigrant indentured to a colonial potter learns his craft.

A young immigrant tries his hand at plumbing, under the watchful eye of an expert in the field.

Citizenship

When the Constitution was adopted, it made certain distinctions between native-born and naturalized citizens. Provision was made for immigration to continue. Immigrants were allowed to hold every office in the land but the highest, the Presidency. And in fact, with the exception of chief justice of the U.S. Supreme Court, immigrants have held every office to which they are entitled.

The first naturalization law, passed by Congress in 1790, provided that "free *white* persons" in the United States for at least two years could be naturalized by the courts. But this meant that immigrant blacks and Asians couldn't be naturalized. And nothing was said about the citizenship status of native-born Americans who were not white. For a long time their status would depend on the state they lived in. Not until 1870 would national citizenship be created.

Native-born American Indians were not recognized as citizens until they were recognized by an act of Congress in 1924. And women, treated as second-class citizens, were denied the right to vote until 1920.

Franklin publicly deplored the presence of so many "German boors" in the colony.

During the crisis of the American Revolution ethnic differences were played down. It helped to create an American, as opposed to an English-American, outlook. Yet America would never overcome ethnic and racial prejudice.

A large Irish family about to step ashore in America

Four

From Ireland and Germany

WHAT DID IMMIGRANTS EXPECT OF LIFE IN THE RAPIDLY CHANGING
America of the 1800s? What were their dreams, their hopes, their illusions?

The Revolutionary War and the War of 1812 curtailed most migration to the United States. But from 1820 to the Civil War the population
grew enormously. In the 1840s the total number of immigrants from all
countries came to nearly 1,750,000. In the 1850s, the figure was
2,500,000. Most entered northern ports—Boston, New York, Philadelphia, with New York receiving the largest share. The Germans moved
west—to Cincinnati, Chicago, St. Louis, Milwaukee. The Irish tended to
remain where they had landed.

By the 1840s two-thirds of the immigrants were looking for wage-
paying work. A third were artisans, and a third were unskilled workers.
The other third were farmers hoping to buy land. Some were attracted by
guidebooks distributed in their homeland by agents of state governments

in America who sought to draw farmers. Industrial workers were especially excited by letters from earlier migrants telling of jobs to be had.

There was often a wide gap between what migrants expected to find in America and the reality. Letters sent home spoke of America as "El Dorado" (the Golden Land). So did the agents of shipping companies who talked of how rich you'd become if you bought a ticket to America. Such talk appealed more to middle class people. Workers simply wanted to find a job, any job, just to survive.

It was famine that caused the huge emigration of Irish to America between 1846 and 1854. Beginning in 1845, a new fungus blighted the potato fields almost annually. Since the Irish depended heavily on the potato for food, when the crops failed, famine set in. People starved by the hundreds.

Gerald Keegan, an Irish schoolteacher who kept a diary in that time, noted the human suffering:

Thousands are dying in a state of total abandonment, without even the luxury of a burial trench. Some have been found dead with grass in their mouth. Dogs and donkeys have become common items of diet. Scores of bodies lie along the roadsides and in abandoned dwellings where they are a prey to the rodents. . . . To lie down and die like cattle in a murrain seemed to be the inevitable fate of most. Two little boys, aged twelve and fourteen, were ordered transported to Australia for seven years for stealing some corn. Hearing these things about our own people makes it hard to preserve the sober use of reason.

Private charities did what they could to help the suffering masses but the British government opposed public aid to the poor, no matter how desperately it was needed.

An Irishman eager to better himself in America studies a poster announcing ship fares.

So boatloads of landless laborers fled to America. Emigration was promoted by landlords who wished to rid their large estates of the helpless, disease-ridden tenants. Tens of thousands died at sea or soon after landing in America.

Ireland's loss was enormous—about 2.25 million people through starvation, disease, and emigration—out of a population of 8 million.

At least 100,000 Irish had already entered the North American colonies before the American Revolution, and more had come in the early 1800s, seeking a better life and freedom from British rule. Most of these were Protestants. Later in the century the stream of immigration became a raging flood. Most came penniless and with little education. Few had trades or industrial skills. The Irish got jobs no one else wanted—cheap day labor, such as building railroads or digging canals. Women worked mostly as domestic servants, paid maybe seventy-five cents a day, with room and board, for putting in sixteen-hour days.

At such low wages, large Irish families were condemned to live in shanties or slums, two or three families holed up in small rooms. Living was a nightmare. Cleanliness, fresh air, and privacy were impossible. Cholera and other diseases erupted.

The worst price paid for such living was borne by the children. More than two out of every three children died before they reached the age of five.

Life for the Irish was made no easier by the widespread prejudice against them. Many of the numerous charitable societies did not extend their aid to the Irish. Irish churches were desecrated and a convent burned. People scorned their nationality, jeered at their customs, manners and speech, ridiculed their faith. They were persecuted, and shut out of occupations and neighborhoods. Prejudice was out in the open: "No Irish Need Apply!" was the standard line in job listings.

An Irish priest, Father John F. Maguire, visited America and wrote about the working women of the Irish American community:

To better the circumstances of her family, the young Irish girl leaves her home for America. There she goes into service, or engages in some kind of feminine employment. The object she has in view . . . protects her from all danger, especially to her character: that object . . . is the welfare of her family, whom she is determined, if possible, to again have with her as of old. To keep her place or retain her employment, what will she not endure?—sneers at her nationality, mockery of her peculiarities, even ridicule of her faith, though the hot blood flushes her cheek with fierce indignation. At every hazard the place must be kept, the money earned, the deposit in savings-bank increased; and though many a night is passed in tears and prayers, her face is calm, her eyes bright, and her voice cheerful.

The arrival of the Irish in the pre–Civil War period triggered an anti-Catholic hysteria. Cries went up of a "foreign conspiracy" engineered by the Pope to seize the United States. Although the Irish were smeared as "brutal" and "clannish," this did not keep the rising industrialists from making use of the cheap plentiful labor they provided. For a generation or more the Irish did the dirtiest and the hardest work. As they climbed the social scale, they were replaced by other ethnic groups, which began to immigrate in large numbers in the 1880s.

The Irish outflow to America went on long after the famine years. But now the poorest were not the first to leave. It was people with skills. In the 1890s alone nearly 400,000 Irish emigrated to America. And almost all stayed, only one out of twelve returned home. Adding it all up, about 4.5 million Irish moved to the United States between 1820 and 1930. Roughly half of all those leaving Ireland in that era were women, usually unmarried, seeking paid work in American cities. By 1900 great numbers of Irish-American women were teaching in the public schools of America's larger cities.

By the close of the nineteenth century, the Irish had won great success in American politics. They had suffered discrimination in Ireland both as Irish and as Catholics, and had strong reason to seek political power to protect themselves. For a long time they focused on local politics. In the twentieth century they achieved great influence in state and national politics as well.

What was the effect of that huge exodus on America? It took a long struggle for the Irish to realize their hopes when they came here. But today the Irish are rated among the most successful of ethnic groups. Measure them by education, income, influence, power, position—they are generally at or near the top. Today, 40 million Americans trace their ancestry to Ireland.

The Germans were the other ethnic group dominating immigration between the 1830s and the 1880s. Together with the Irish they made up almost 7 out of 10 foreign-born in 1860. But there were major differences between the two. The Germans spoke a foreign language and represented three religious groups—Protestants, Catholics, and Jews. Most of them migrated in family groups, and more of them returned home. The Germans came largely for economic reasons rather than because of a crisis such as the famine. The Irish took no pride in their government which was run by British overlords. But the Germans were proud of their country's achievements, especially after the separate German states were unified into the German Empire in 1871.

It was the modernizing of Germany in the mid-1800s that led Germans to migrate. Rapid industrialization and urbanization created political and social changes that made it hard to continue the old ways of life.

In Germany's rural districts women especially found life almost unendurable. Female farm laborers earned half what the men were paid. That made it much harder for them to scrape together the money to emigrate. An American consul in the Thuringia district describes their life:

Prejudices against Irish and German immigrants led to the formation of the political party called the Know Nothings. This nasty cartoon of 1850 charges the immigrants with being drunkards who steal American elections.

American readers will hardly understand how it can be that the severest part of existence in this whole region falls to the lot of woman. But such is the fact. She is the servant and the burden-bearer. . . . The position of wife and mother appears to shield her from no hardship. . . . Her sex is liberally represented in most of the manual-labor occupations of the district, even to mining and foundry work, but far less liberally in any branch of clerical or professional life. . . .

Thus it is seen that the chief pursuits of women in this district are not of a gentle or refining character. They perform by far the greater part of all the out-door manual service. The planting and the sowing, including the preparation of the soil therefor, is done by them. I have seen many a woman in the past few weeks holding the plow drawn by a pair of cows, and still more of them "toting" manure into the fields in baskets strapped to their backs. They also do the haying, including the mowing and the pitching; likewise the harvesting; after which they thresh much of the grain with the old-fashioned hand flail. They accompany the coal carts through the city and put the coal in the cellars, while the male driver sits upon his seat. They carry on nearly all the dairy business, and draw the milk into town in a hand cart—a woman and a dog usually constituting the team. "I have just written to my wife," said [an American traveler recently], "that it is a very serious thing to be a dog in Germany, or a cow, or a woman."

When obliged to seek new jobs many Germans preferred to try life overseas. And now it had become easier to move, what with the new steamboats and railways. Bremen and Hamburg became major ports in the emigrant trade. They carried the Germans chiefly to New York.

Far more Germans than Irish worked at skilled trades. They were found in the lager beer industry, built on German capital and skilled labor. Germans were active too as bakers, butchers, cigarmakers, distillers, machinists, cabinetmakers, tailors. Still others entered business and the professions.

Fewer German women entered the labor force than did other women, either immigrant or native-born. Those who did generally didn't seek factory or clerical jobs but moved into the service sector as nurses, peddlers, tailors, saloonkeepers, bakers. Many created family businesses within their communities.

Immigrant girls as young as eleven or twelve often found work as day help in Yankee families. Such domestic work placed them in intimate contact with middle-class American home life. They learned English rapidly, absorbing American attitudes too, and adopting American dress. So these girls not only became Americanized quickly but as they got older, passed their new American values on to their children. The adjustment was faster for them than for young Germans who lived and worked in heavily German cities, such as Milwaukee, where they were steeped in the German language and culture.

German immigrants set a good record as farmers. They tended to settle in rural smalltown areas. By 1870 one in four was engaged in agriculture. Sometimes there were enough Germans living near one another for their language to stay in use into the fourth and fifth generations.

Most German migrants of the nineteenth century were Protestants, usually Lutherans; a third of the immigrants were Catholic; and the others were Jews. It was the east coast, especially New York, that drew most Jews. Within Germany Jews generally had lived in small cities and market towns and were artisans, petty traders, and cattle dealers. A small number were merchants, and very few, bankers. They left home for the same reasons as the others, but with the additional desire to escape discriminatory taxation and laws that limited their basic human rights.

The rate of return to Germany for non-Jews was about one in seven or eight; for Jews it was less than one in twenty.

Few German Jews in America were artisans, and of these most were tailors. Far more built their livelihood in retail trades. Some moved up from roving peddler to a retail or wholesale business and even developed great department stores and chains. "More of the first-generation entered into business or other middle-class occupations than any other nineteenth-century immigrant group," according to the historian Roger Daniels. He notes that a major difference between German Jews and other German immigrants was that "as Jews, they faced a double prejudice, since, in addition to being foreigners, they were not Christians."

Men in War

German Americans have played a great role in America's military history, as well as its cultural life. Back in the days of the American Revolution, Baron von Steuben arrived from Germany to mold George Washington's motley military forces into an effective army. General Carl Schurz and General Franz Sigel helped the Union forces win the Civil War. General John J. Pershing commanded the American armies in World War I, and General Dwight D. Eisenhower led the army that conquered the Nazis in World War II. In that same war, Admiral Chester Nimitz commanded the Pacific Fleet that defeated the Japanese and General Carl Spaatz the bombers that devastated much of Germany. General Norman Schwarzkopf led the American and allied forces in the Persian Gulf War of 1991.

During the "century of immigration," 1820–1924, about six million Germans entered the United States. They were the largest single immigrant and ethnic group. German Americans—many of them middle class, urban graduates of universities—created and maintained the most extraordinary cultural program of any immigrant group. By the 1880s they had established some eight hundred German language newspapers, seventy of them

Many German immigrants moved to the upper Midwest. Some entered such grueling occupations as logging, shown here in a Minnesota snow scene.

Attention Workingmen!

══ GREAT ══
MASS-MEETING

TO-NIGHT, at 7.30 o'clock,
═══ AT THE ═══
HAYMARKET, Randolph St, Bet. Desplaines and Halsted.

Good Speakers will be present to denounce the latest atrocious act of the police, the shooting of our fellow-workmen yesterday afternoon.

Workingmen Arm Yourselves and Appear in Full Force!
THE EXECUTIVE COMMITTEE

Achtung, Arbeiter!

Große
Maffen-Verfammlung

Heute Abend, ½8 Uhr, auf dem
Heumarkt, Randolph-Straße, zwischen Desplaines- u. Halsted-Str.

☞ Gute Redner werden den neuesten Schurkenstreich der Polizei, indem sie gestern Nachmittag unsere Brüder erschoß, geißeln.

☞ Arbeiter, bewaffnet Euch und erscheint massenhaft!
Das Executiv-Comite.

dailies. In many cities and states with large German-speaking populations the German language was taught in both public and parochial schools. They maintained singing societies, symphony orchestras, literary clubs, and a high profile in the world of sports.

Sadly, when America entered World War I in 1917, joining the Allies to fight against Germany, President Woodrow Wilson's propaganda mill spread the virus of fear. Wilson himself attacked "hyphenated Americans," accusing them of pouring "the poison of disloyalty into the very arteries of our national life," and calling for "such creatures" to be "crushed out."

Before the outbreak of the war, German Americans had been highly praised as among our most worthy citizens. Now a mindless anger raged so fiercely against them that people feared to speak German in public. The teaching of German was forbidden not only in high schools but at some colleges and universities, too. Anti-German hysteria forced many of German America's cultural institutions to shut down.

A handbill in both German and English calling workers to a labor protest rally at Haymarket Square in Chicago on May 4, 1886. A riot eventually broke out, after someone threw a bomb that fatally injured seven policemen and one spectator.

Even the elderly, such as this Russian Jewish immigrant at Ellis Island, found persecution in Czarist Russia so intolerable they fled to America.

Five

Out of Eastern Europe

ANTI-SEMITISM WAS AN ANCIENT TRADITION IN RUSSIA. UNDER THE CZARS who ruled Russia for almost four centuries, Jews were hounded and humiliated by hundreds of restrictions. Military conscription of Jews was particularly heavy. Boys were drafted into the army for twenty-five years of service. Whatever the Russian people suffered—poverty, hunger, misfortune—was always blamed on the Jews.

The Russian way of "solving the Jewish problem" was to treat them like the plague. From 1804 Jews were forced to live in a confined region called the Pale of Settlement. This was a rigid policy of segregation designed to save the "Holy" Russian people from contamination by the Jews. Within that Pale, Jews were tied to shtetls, market towns where Jews provided services to the local peasants. They ran shops, and peddled goods. They administered mills, taverns, inns. They worked as cobblers, cabinetmakers, metalworkers, weavers, bakers, tanners, watchmakers.

In the 1860s broad economic changes began to affect Eastern Europe. The expanding railway system brought the products of urban factories to the Pale, replacing the handwork of Jewish artisans. Trains also brought cheaper grain from faraway markets, weakening the peasant economy that sustained the shtetls. In the cities, commercial and financial enterprises flourished, undermining shtetl merchants and moneylenders. Artisans—tailors, cobblers, hatmakers—saw the need for their skills disappear, and they sank into poverty and beggary. Half the people in some shtetls had to rely on charity to survive. Making things worse was the great rise in the Jewish population. It jumped from one million Jews in the Pale in 1800, to four million in 1880.

Some Jews left their stricken villages and towns to seek work in the new industrial centers of Warsaw, Lodz, Bialystok, and Grodno—all cities within the Pale. A few others went beyond, to the magical land of America.

But everything changed in 1881. That was the year Czar Alexander II was assassinated. The false charge that the Jews had plotted his death was rumored everywhere. Pogroms—the organized massacre of helpless people—broke out by the hundreds, and thousands of Jews were injured or killed. The government did nothing to halt the pogroms and at times instigated them. They charged the Russian peasants and workers had been enslaved by Jews and were rising up against their exploiters.

The truth of course was that the economic misery of the Russian people was the inevitable result of the brutal serfdom in which Russia's rulers had held them for centuries, long after the rest of Europe was moving into modern times. To divert the blame for oppression, the czar, the nobility, and the landlords made the Jews the scapegoat. Such violent outbreaks against the Jews were ancient history in Russia. One of the earliest on record goes back to 1113, when the Jews of Kiev were attacked and pillaged.

Beyond these reasons for migration there were other causes. One of these was *takhlis*—a unique guiding principle of East European Jewish

Russian emigrants awaiting the ship that will take them to America

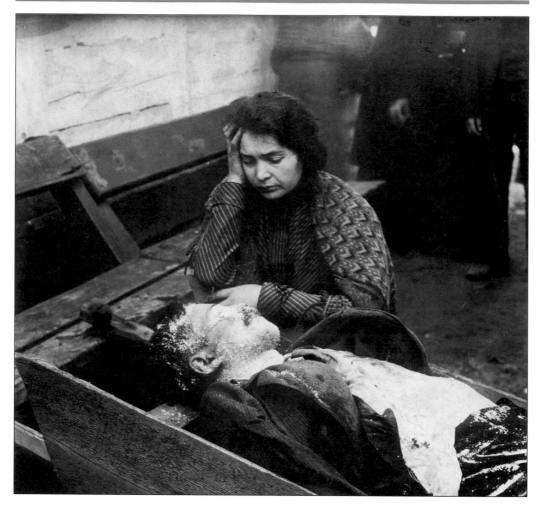

A woman mourns over the victim of a pogrom, one of many savage attacks on Russian Jews launched by mobs with government approval. To escape poverty and persecution, millions fled to the United States.

life. It means you will not be satified by merely living; you must try to achieve something. It might be status or prestige in religious or intellectual life. It might be financial security. But in the ghetto so many barriers to achievement existed that your hopes for *takhlis* were small. To many the only way out seemed to be migration to America. There, it was said,

46

you could make something of yourself, work your way up, realize your potential, educate your children to make their mark in the world.

The 1880s saw the beginning of a mass migration from Russia. At first in a trickle, then in a torrent. Four million Jews left Eastern Europe between 1880 and 1924. Over three million of them came to the United States. Because of that heavy migration, the Jewish population of the United States increased at a more rapid rate during this period than the population as a whole. The vast majority of Americans of Jewish descent today stem from that immigration.

The Merlin family is an example of how whole families migrated. They came from Dubrovna, a village on the banks of the Dnieper River in Russia. They were weavers of prayer shawls, desperate to escape oppression piled on top of poverty. Two young brothers, Beryl and Michel, came first. They earned a living by peddling notions in small towns outside Atlanta, Georgia. They saved money to buy ship tickets to send back to their family in Dubrovna. And then, wrote Michel:

Gradually our family came across the ocean to us. Finally we had with us our mother, our sister, and our five other brothers, including Lazear Ari with his wife and four children. We were all happy. The whole family was here.

By now [after World War I] there were about 100 Dubrovners in Atlanta. We sent money to Dubrovna after the war, each to his own people. Once we sent a very large sum of money through the new Soviet government, to the entire population of Dubrovna, the *goyim* as well as the Jews, so as not to create bad feelings towards the Jews there. Later we learned from a Russian visitor that the government said it knew better who was in need. . . .

All of us are truly happy and lucky that we ran away from Russia and came to the new and free America. America, be blessed for all the good that you gave to us.

Next door to Russia was the dual monarchy of Austria and Hungary. That sprawling empire too was a producer of emigrants—many of them were rural artisans and peasants who set out to find a better life in America. Hungary knew appalling inequalities in land distribution. A few thousand families owned about 50 percent of all the land. A boom in population made it hard for young people to find work.

In the regions of Austrian Galicia and Bukovina emigration became intense. There were more farm hands and day laborers depending on the land for a living than agriculture could support. People emigrated from almost every village. Between 1880 and 1910 at least 10 percent of the Galicians emigrated.

Serbs too departed, finding it increasingly hard to survive on small plots of land. And the underdeveloped industry of the empire forced Slavs to look elsewhere to make ends meet. Slovaks, Poles, and others in this complex empire had similar reasons to leave home and head for America.

The huge estates of Austro-Hungary in the hands of the aristocracy were worked by tenants, sharecroppers, and day laborers. Most of them formed a landless class, who found seasonal work for only 150 to 200 days a year. A researcher reported:

Their standard way of life was one of slow starvation. They lived in unhygienic, over-crowded slums, on an average yearly income of hardly more than a hundred dollars. Children were underfed. There was usury, and compulsory labor for women; 96 percent of the farm servants lived in buildings which also housed stables. Disease was rampant; tuberculosis ravaged the countryside, and infant mortality was very high.

The government in Vienna passed no laws to halt emigration. But the ruling political and economic class had the newspapers print stories

A Slovak mother poses with her children on Ellis Island, hoping to find work in America that would end the slow starvation she knew back home.

Two young Polish peasant women, clutching all their belongings, prepare to leave Ellis Island.

of the bitter experiences of immigrants working in the mines and foundries of America. To little effect, for most of the rural folk seldom got hold of a paper and didn't read much besides the Bible and little booklets of the lives of the saints. This gave a propagandist the idea of creating cheap short booklets telling "true stories" of the poor, miserable life of the empire's immigrants in America. Preachers and teachers too were asked to help spread a negative image of America.

It didn't work. About 1.5 million people coming from Austro-Hungary landed in the United States in the four decades preceding World War I. The majority were young men, but an increasing number were women.

What countered the bad reports of American life were the personal messages sent home by relatives or friends. The greatest attraction the rural people came to see in emigration was the money that could be earned in America. Studies show that the majority of emigrants did not want to break permanently with their communities. Their aim was to earn better wages, and to send or bring money home. In their rural homeland a day laborer's wages, if a person was lucky enough to get hired, were hardly enough to support a family. No wonder the wages in an American factory appeared fabulous to them. "You can get rich quickly," they believed.

An Italian family looking for lost baggage on Ellis Island

Six

From Italy
and Beyond

Out of Italy in the years between 1880 and 1920 came 4.2 million people bound for the United States. No other ethnic group sent so many immigrants in such a short time. Italy, a newly unified kingdom in 1870, had a population of 28 million. The kingdom was divided by conflict between church and state, north and south, modern urban industry and near-feudal rural poverty. Before the 1870s scattered groups of Italians had left their country; most went not to the Untied States but to Argentina or Brazil.

During America's colonial times and its early years as a nation the Italians who came were mostly artisans, merchants, musicians, actors, sailors, doctors. Some Italian migrants contributed to America's musical life. The best known, arriving in 1805, was Lorenzo da Ponte, a Venetian who had written the librettos for three of Mozart's greatest operas.

Italy had its peasant south and its industrialized north. Both regions contributed to migration. But most Italians entering the port of New York were refugees from southern Italy. In their region a handful of aristocrats owned most of the land and had been squeezing profit out of peasant tenants for centuries. They were a tiny ruling elite indifferent to introducing improvements in agricultural tools and methods. The peasants still labored with wooden plows much as their Roman ancestors had done.

Illiteracy in southern Italy was perhaps the highest in Europe. Housing was terrible, there were no public welfare programs, people barely got by on a limited diet. And if that weren't bad enough, the land also suffered from deforestation and soil erosion, and the people from earthquakes and malaria.

When Italy completed its unification in 1870, northerners dominated the new nation. They looked down on the southerners as barbarians, fit only for exploitation. The northerner-dominated government failed to provide roads or schools, and was ingenious only in creating more taxes. Overpopulation, as in eastern Europe, mounted steadily, the total population rising 25 percent in the last quarter of the 1800s. With a surplus population, unemployment, diseases, oppression, and neglect, what reason was there to stay home? Slowly farmers, laborers and artisans began to head for the United States.

They were ready to take a chance on life in an unknown country across the Atlantic. America, they heard, would improve their children's future, provide dowries for their daughters, and educate their sons. Letters sent to their villages from America told them New York's tenements were crowded, but they also heard that their village life was recreated in neighborhoods full of their own people.

Again, for Italians, as for other people, it was not the poorest and the most desperate who chose to migrate, but enterprising people able to make such decisions. The sons and daughters of small land-holders, the upwardly mobile tenant farmers and their children, took passage in steer-

Beginning with Columbus

Hundreds of Italians took part in the exploration of North America. Most were serving France or Spain, however, and they founded no New Italy here. No doubt because in their time there was no Italy in a national sense. Remember that it was a Genoese—Columbus—who "discovered" America, and a Florentine, Amerigo Vespucci, who gave America its name. A Venetian, Giovanni Caboto, "discovered" New England and it was another Florentine navigator, Giovanni da Verrazano, who first sailed into New York Harbor and for whom the great bridge across the Narrows is named.

age. So did artisans and small businessmen. They would adapt easily to the United States.

Three-fourths of the Italian emigrants were male, mostly in their working years. Their return rate was quite high, somewhere between 30 and 50 percent. They returned not for any love of their nation, for modern Italian nationalism developed only slowly. Instead, their strongest ties were to their families and neighbors. When they came back, they came back not as failures but bringing money. By this time moving back and forth to the United States was a relatively short voyage, and seasonal work on railroads or in construction in the United States provided quick

Italian laborers dig a culvert for the electric railway running through the Lebanon Valley of New York around 1900.

cash wages. Women and children came back, as well as men.

As one historian puts it, "The migration was a reasonable and traditional response of a clever people to adverse conditions and attractive opportunities." Italians formed one of the largest migration movements in the modern world. They made up about 10 percent of global migrations between 1830 and 1930: 27 million Italians on the move.

Compared with the masses of other ethnic immigrants, the immigrants from Scandinavia were considerably fewer. They came mostly from the rural parts of Sweden, Norway, and Denmark, and they were almost entirely Protestant. Between 1820 and 1920 about 2,200,000 Scandinavians arrived in the United States. (Only 125,000 came before the Civil War.)

The Swedes were the largest contingent—small farmers, artisans—and usually came in family groups. Some of these people left home seeking more religious freedom than the Lutheran church was willing to allow, but most of them were seeking economic opportunities. When Sweden's population expanded rapidly in the 1800s, less land was available for farming. A severe famine in the late 1860s caused Swedish emigration to surge. Many people settled in the wheat belt of the American Midwest. Later arrivals moved into the Pacific Northwest.

But not all Swedes wanted to farm. A significant minority were urban folk. They made Chicago the second largest Swedish city in the world. And city life was hard on these immigrants. Cholera epidemics ravaged the city almost every summer, hitting the poor the worst. Most of Chicago's Swedes worked for wages. They played a big part in the labor force, the men chiefly as skilled and unskilled workers, the women as domestic servants and textile mill hands.

The Swedes, like most immigrants to America, settled in ethnic enclaves. Today they are often recalled as ghettos and viewed as bad. But in the past they were an important waystation for immigrants on the path to fuller assimilation into American life. Isador Kjellberg, a Swedish American journalist, wrote in 1890:

> The liveliest section of the busy Chicago Avenue shows its entire length, a large mass of exclusively Swedish signs, that Anderson, Petterson, and Lundstrom were here conducting a Swedish general store, a Swedish bookshop, a Swedish beer saloon . . . and so on.

And wherever one goes one hears Swedish sounds generally, and if one's thoughts are somewhat occupied, one can believe one has been quickly transported back to Sweden.

Norway, another part of Scandinavia, was under Danish rule for hundreds of years. In 1814 it declared its independence, but after brief conflict with Sweden it was agreed that Sweden's king would also be king of Norway. That shaky union lasted until 1905, when Norway got a king of its own.

Only 3 or 4 percent of Norway's land was tillable. Yet two-thirds of the people lived in rural areas. As the birthrate rose, the majority of the rural folk became landless. So Norwegians migrated to the American countryside where land was abundant and cheap. The largest number came after the American Civil War, flocking to where earlier arrivals had already settled. Over half of the Norwegian Americans at the peak of migration lived in Wisconsin, Minnesota, and North Dakota. Norwegians were so heavily concentrated in these three states that they were called "a nation within a nation."

In the last quarter of the nineteenth century more Norwegians came alone than in families, and some chose to live in cities, not on farms. The largest number picked Brooklyn, where they found work in the maritime trades.

In the late 1860s at least sixty Norwegian ships a week entered New York harbor, and some 50,000 crew members "emigrated" to the United States simply by walking off their ships. Many found work in the American merchant marine, on both coasts and on the Great Lakes.

The smallest of the Scandinavian groups were the Danes. Very few of them left home before the era of mass emigration. One of these was Jonas Bronck, who in the 1600s bought the large area north and east of Manhattan now called the Bronx, named after him. Another was a black-

This Norwegian woman sits before her family's sod home in Minnesota.

smith from Copenhagen—Peter Lassen—an early explorer of the West for whom a California mountain is named.

The first large group of Danes were 20,000 Mormon converts who settled in the valley of the Great Salt Lake in Utah in the latter part of the

Greek immigrants gather for a group portrait at Ellis Island. Note that they are all male.

1800s. Also, several small Danish socialist groups tried unsuccessfully to plant settlements in the West.

But it was economic forces that led the great majority of the 300,000 Danish immigrants to go to America. They were mostly young males, about half of them from rural Denmark, the others from towns and cities.

Behind them they left many young women who would never marry or bear children. The great majority of emigrants came from the lower ranks of society. The largest group were rural laborers, but industrial workers, craftsmen and tradesmen, and some professionals also made the journey.

Many Danes came with specific destinations in mind. This indicates they had connections, had been invited to come by someone they knew. The flow of money ran two ways: the immigrants sent some home, but the stay-at-homes sent money to America when hard times hit family or friends.

Although Italy sent more people to America than any other Mediterranean group, the Greeks emigrated too. About 600,000 Greeks came between 1890 and 1924. A third of these were from Greece itself, while the other two-thirds came from Turkey. (Note that back then more Greeks lived outside Greece—in the Balkans, in Turkey, and in Egypt.)

Almost all the Greek immigrants chose work in the cities. They shunned farming because back home it had brought them only misery and hardship. Most settled in the northeast and north central states, although a large number went to California. A smaller group, from the Greek islands, went to the west coast of Florida where they pursued sponge fishing.

Greeks found openings in both heavy and light industry. They worked on railroad construction gangs, in textile mills, meatpacking, mining. A good many opened small businesses, such as flower shops and inexpensive restaurants. Few got rich on such enterprises, and many failed. One field Greeks pioneered and prospered in was the motion picture industry. They built both theater chains and film production companies.

Wedding photo of Benjamin and Mary Meltzer (parents of the author), who came to America around the turn of the century as young immigrants from Austro-Hungary

Seven

Across the Atlantic
in Steerage

UNTIL 1882 ALMOST ANYONE COULD ENTER AMERICA. U.S. GOVERNMENT policy had been "hands off." Immigrants could come as they pleased and nothing was done to encourage or discourage them. That year Congress adopted the first national immigration law. Inspection of immigrants was to be carried out by state boards at all ports of entry. Undesirables were to be kept out. Persons to be turned back included prostitutes, Chinese "coolies," or "any convicts, lunatics, idiots or any person unable to take care of himself without becoming a public charge."

Shipping lines were taxed fifty cents per immigrant to cover the costs of running landing depots and attached hospitals. Seven out of every ten arrivals came through the port of New York; the others entered at Portland, Boston, Philadelphia, Baltimore, Key West, New Orleans, Galveston, and San Francisco.

Investors looking for new sources of profit saw a golden opportunity in the rising tide of emigration from Europe. Railways and steamships were improved and expanded to meet the need. The time required for a transatlantic crossing was reduced to days rather than weeks. The leading European passenger lines set up networks of ticket agents to reach every possible buyer. By 1907 four ports of departure—Naples, Liverpool, Bremen, and Hamburg—had cornered 60 percent of the trade. In that year alone 1.25 million immigrants entered the United States.

Conditions for travelers improved somewhat under the pressure of competition. The major shipping lines—German and British—opened dormitories in their ports to house, feed, and medically check the passengers waiting for the next ship. The price of tickets gradually dropped. But when some critics pointed to the dismal conditions for the poorest passengers in steerage, arrogant officials replied that "those people" weren't used to anything better and wouldn't appreciate it. And besides, were the crowded tenements they were going to any better?

What was it like to take passage in steerage? My grandfather's experience gives us some idea. I'm sure his story was much like that of any other immigrant in the late nineteenth century. Samuel Richter, at the age of twenty-seven, had a wife, Rose, and seven children. They lived in Skoryki, a village in the vast Austro-Hungarian empire. How he earned a living I don't know. It couldn't have been much of a living, for in 1895, thinking no doubt that in America he could do better for his family, he said goodbye to Rose and the seven kids, and crossed a strange land for a distant seaport. He was ready to risk a harsh voyage across the Atlantic and start life over again in the unknown world of New York.

He crossed the Atlantic in steerage, the cheapest class on the steamship. He slept way below deck in a compartment that held about three hundred immigrants. The berths, in two tiers, were six feet two inches long, with a two-and-a-half foot space above each berth. The iron framework held a mattress and a pillow stuffed with straw or seaweed. His blanket was so flimsy that he had to sleep in his clothing to keep warm.

To help pass time on the long voyage to America these immigrants formed a musical band.

The voyage lasted sixteen days, but no steward ever cleaned his berth. There was no room for hand baggage. The few things he carried from home—a pot, teakettle, an embroidered pillowcase Rose had made for him—he kept in his berth. (The floor was forbidden.) He had no closet or hooks; everything he was not wearing had to be piled on the narrow berth. Even the eating utensils supplied by the shipping line had to be tucked under the mattress.

No dining room was provided for steerage passengers. Samuel lined up with the others for his food and ate it in his berth. There were no wastebaskets or sickness cans; the steerage floor was always damp and filthy and the air stank sickeningly. The food? A chunk of white bread that tasted like chalk and a smelly herring. (He would not touch the nonkosher meat or soup.) After two days of that diet, he dug into the hardtack and the rocklike farmer cheese he had been advised to stow in his pack. When a storm came up on the fourth day, he didn't need food. He had plenty to give up as the ship rocked and shook.

Privacy was for the aristocrats on the upper decks. Down below, the men, women, and children were all mixed together. A shy man, Samuel glanced away when his neighbors took off their clothing. He stayed in what he wore the day he boarded ship.

They all suffered for lack of water. Just one small cup was handed out each evening, and it had to do for twenty-four hours. Samuel learned you could buy more water but he couldn't spare a penny. By evening, he often burned with thirst, and couldn't save until morning the cupful handed to him. After a week at sea, his energy gone, his spirits low, he wondered why he had done this crazy thing. He lay on his bunk in a stupor. When his stomach churned and he needed the toilet he had to wait in a long line. There were only eight toilets and eight washbasins for about 250

The photographer Alfred Stieglitz gives us this glimpse into steerage on one of the Atlantic steamships.

Eager immigrants crowd the steerage deck as the S. S. Hamburg *enters New York harbor.*

women and children, and the same ratio for the men. When he finally got into the washroom, the toilet seats were wet and water stood inches deep on the floor. Samuel had to get up by five in the morning or even earlier to use the washroom before breakfast, which was at seven. After a few days, he gave up trying to stay clean. There was no bathtub or shower, and if he stayed at a washbasin for more than a few seconds, a growl of anger went up from the line behind him.

But one day, at last, his ship steamed into New York harbor and he felt the heavy blanket of depression lift. He drank in the rich green of Staten Island and the soft blue of sky and sea, the bustle of the boats hurrying across the bay, the floating, many-windowed palaces he learned were ferries.

The immigrants on Samuel's ship were taken off in small boats, each group numbered and lettered so that when they arrived at the immigration reception center on Ellis Island, "the man with the pen who asks the questions" could match them against the passenger list. Samuel waited in a little stall with the others in his group, all huddled together, sweating in fear and anxiety. Would they be let in or turned back?

Samuel went through the admission process without a hitch, the doctor gave him a clean bill of health, and he was admitted. His ordeal was over. A few minutes later he sat in a big waiting room, eating his first decent meal in weeks. Then the ferry carried him to Battery Park at the tip of Manhattan.

Lining up at Ellis Island to be registered

Eight

Through Ellis Island

New York was the chief port of entry for a great many of the immigrant groups we've described. Between 1820 and 1839 over half a million entered the port. In the next twenty years, however, 4.5 million emigrants arrived: 40 percent were Irish, 32 percent were German, and 16 percent English. Three out of every four newcomers entered at New York.

In the early 1840s about forty passenger ships every day dropped anchor off Manhattan. The biggest carried a thousand men, women, and children in steerage. Their passengers plunged into chaos, many falling sick or dying of diseases contracted aboard the crowded ships. And as soon as they touched land, predatory men began cheating them out of what little money they had by offering help in finding housing and work—but the help never arrived.

Reformers prevailed on the state legislature to reorganize the immigration process—inspecting ships on arrival, providing emergency medical aid for those arriving sick and destitute, and arranging food, clothing, and shelter for those urgently in need.

In 1855 Castle Garden, once an old fort on a tiny island just off the Battery at the foot of Manhattan, was converted into the nation's first immigrant reception center. It was run by the state, not the federal government. It reduced the abuses immigrants had suffered for so long. After ships passed through a quarantine station six miles south of the city, they anchored off the Castle Garden pier. Medical officers and customs officials came aboard to inspect the passengers, who were then barged to the landing depot.

What was it like for an immigrant to enter America by this door? I. Kopeloff, a young Russian Jew, tells us:

Castle Garden, a large circular, rotunda-shaped building, had the appearance, to my eyes, of the arsenal in the castle of Boberisk, or of its tower, and struck me with gloom. . . . The main hall was huge and barren, and gave off an uncanny coldness which produced in its inhabitants an involuntary oppression. One after another sighed and sighed. . . . [It] was often so crowded, so jammed, that there was simply nowhere to sit by day, or any place to lie down at night—not even on the bare floor.

The filth was unendurable, so many packages, pillows, featherbeds and foul clothing (often just plain rags) that each immigrant had dragged with him over the seas and clung to as if they were precious—all of this provided great opportunity for vermin, those filthy little beasts, that crawled about freely and openly over the clutter and made life disagreeable. The constant scratching and the distress of the little children touched one to the quick.

At Castle Garden, immigration clerks supervised baggage collection, steered travelers desiring to go beyond the city to approved agents of railroad and steamship companies, and kept an eye out for crooks and con men. A labor official directed unskilled newcomers to points inland for work on farms and construction crews, in factories and mines, and as laborers and domestic servants.

The new arrivals who chose to stay in the city would transform every aspect of life in New York—its patterns of work, housing, religion, politics. The great mass of them entered the working class. By the late 1850s New York's predominantly Anglo-Protestant middle and upper classes would rest on the foundation of a working class three-fourths of whom were foreigners.

The old state-run entry system caved in under the enormous pressure of ever higher waves of immigration. Complaints piled up until the federal government decided to dispense with state control, take over the immigration process, and build a new center for New York.

To replace Castle Garden the government chose a tiny blob of mud and sand lying in a shallow of New York Harbor. Workers doubled the three acres of Ellis Island with landfill in order to provide space for a large building. The two-story station made of wood was about 400 by 150 feet, and looked like a seaside hotel. Opened on January 1, 1892, this firetrap burned down in 1897 (no one was injured, luckily). It was replaced in 1900 with a new brick building. Again the planners guessed wrong, for they never expected the half-million annual immigration rate of the recent past would climb even higher. It did. For the next fifteen years the newcomers had to fight fiercely for room even though the island was eventually expanded to an area of twenty-one acres.

Flanking the main building on Ellis Island were medical facilities, a bathhouse, laundry, kitchen, dining room, and an electric power plant. With the new facilities came new regulations. The 1882 law was replaced with a broader one in 1891. There were new categories of "undesirables"—polygamists, people guilty of "moral turpitude," and people suffering from "a loathsome or contagious disease." A law of 1885, intended to keep out

At this medical inspection, eyes are examined to make sure no one with trachoma, a contagious eye infection, is admitted.

A New York City health officer checks for signs of typhoid fever, at the time of an epidemic scare.

workers brought over under contract to employers, was toughened. Aliens who came in illegally or who became public charges within a year of arrival were to be deported. The 1891 law was stiffened two years later by amendments.

On any one day Ellis Island might handle as many as 7,000 immigrants. How was this possible? Jacob Riis, a reporter-photographer, watched the newcomers in 1903 and told what he saw in *Century* magazine:

By the time the lighters are tied up at the Ellis Island wharf their human cargo is numbered and lettered in groups that correspond with like entries in the manifest, and so are marshaled upon and over the bridge that leads straight into the United States to the man with the pen who asks questions. When the crowd is great and pressing, they camp by squads in little stalls bearing their proprietary stamp, as it were, finding one another and being found when astray by the mystic letter that brings together in the close companionship of a common peril—the pen, one stroke of which can shut the gate against them—men and women who in another hour go their way, very likely never to meet or hear of one another again on earth. The sense of the impending trial sits visibly upon the waiting crowd. Here and there a masterful spirit strides boldly on; the mass huddle close, with more or less anxious look. Five minutes after it is over, eating their dinner in the big waiting-room, they present an entirely different appearance. Signs and numbers have disappeared. The groups are recasting themselves on lines of nationality and personal preference. . . .

Behind carefully guarded doors wait the "outs," the detained immigrants, for the word that will let down the bars or fix them in place immovably. The guard is for a double purpose: that no one shall enter or leave the detention room. . . . And the hopelessly bewildered are there, often enough exasperated at the restraint, which they cannot understand, waiting for friends able to keep them. . .

Harsh and discomforting as the inspection system at Ellis Island seemed to the immigrants, still, it was relatively efficient. In comparison, the other major immigration ports were understaffed and chaotic.

New arrivals wait in the huge dining hall for a meal.

Greed and inhumanity may be blamed for many abuses of the immigrants. As aliens, they had little or no protection against fraud. They responded eagerly to friendly gestures, thinking everyone in this wonderland must be glad to help. Countless thousands were cheated at docks and on trains and boats, and suffered painful losses at the hands of dishonest travel agents, lawyers, bankers, notaries, interpreters. We admit you, the U.S. government said in effect; now you're on your own.

A mother and her children work in their tenement room making wreaths, trying to eke out the father's pitifully low wages.

Nine

Sweatshops
and Slums

THE GREAT WAVE OF IMMIGRATION THAT SWEPT INTO THE UNITED STATES in the late nineteenth century was a powerful force in reshaping society. A diverse working class emerged, made up of men, women, and children from all points of the compass. Skilled workers—one sixth of the work-force—were usually white men, and either native-born or the descendants of northern and western European immigrants. Most of them got their jobs through family and friends. Skilled workers, who enjoyed high wages, demanded respect from their bosses and were likely to form and join unions.

What happened in 1912 in Lawrence, Massachusetts, the largest textile town in the world, is an example of how militant immigrant labor could become when they decided they would no longer take abuse. Ray Stannard Baker, an investigative reporter, went to Lawrence to cover the mass revolt:

Upon that day, in the Washington mill of the so-called Woolen Trust, a handful of Italian operatives had gone to draw their pay envelopes. Of all the mingled peoples of Lawrence, none are so humble as the Italians, none so eager for work at any price, and none so ill-paid. They are the last and the poorest of the successive waves of people from Europe which have been surging upon our shores during the last thirty years. When these people opened their envelopes, they found that there was a reduction of pay corresponding to two hours of work in a week—the price, perhaps, of three or four loaves of bread. A small matter, indeed, the comfortably fed outsider may observe, but in Lawrence, where many adult workers make only $6 to $7.50 a week, it is not an unimportant matter. A matter, indeed, of very great importance!

"It was like a spark of electricity," an overseer described it to me.

It changed instantly the discipline of years: it brought about sudden wild confusion. One of the bosses, attempting to restore order with the threat formerly as potent as magic, shouted to one of the Italians:

"Tony, if you don't get back to your place, you'll lose your job."

"To hell with the job," responded Tony. "I'll pitch it."

And "pitch it" they did. They swept out of the mill, taking hundreds of others with them, they marched to other mills and called out hundreds more. On the way a few belts were cut, a few windows broken—losses not serious in themselves, but symbolic of the temper of the men, suggestive of future possibilities. And with marching and singing through the main streets of the town the strike began.

The unskilled workers were usually eastern and southern European or Chinese immigrants, or African Americans. Poorly paid and insecure, they barely kept their heads above the poverty line. Many earned only

$1.50 a day, if they were lucky enough to find day labor. Whether skilled or not, they all faced the constant threat of unemployment. The business cycle of ups and downs laid a terrible burden on working people when depressions struck.

Industry systematically hired immigrants. Why? A report on the Carnegie Steel Company, issued by the Sage Foundation, gave these reasons:

> Their habit of silent submission . . . and their willingness to work long hours and overtime without a murmur. Foreigners as a rule earn the lowest wages and work the full stint of hours.
>
> Many work in intense heat, the din of machinery and the noise of escaping steam. The congested conditions of the plants add to the physical discomforts . . . while their ignorance of the language and of modern machinery increases the risk. How many of the Slavs, Lithuanians and Italians are injured in Pittsburgh in one year is unknown. . . . When I mentioned a plant that had a bad reputation to a priest he said, "Oh, that is the slaughterhouse; they kill them there every day."

Andrew Carnegie, owner of the steel mills, and himself a Scottish immigrant, had his workers put in twelve hours a day, seven days a week, including Sundays.

Plant owners used many of the immigrants as strikebreakers. Swedish, German and Italian immigrants were brought into the coal fields in the 1870s and 1880s to break strikes. The differences in language and culture made it hard for the unions to organize the newcomers. Employers encouraged constant war among ethnic groups.

Nevertheless workers continued to organize and strike for better wages and working conditions. In 1886 an Italian worker in a silk mill of New Jersey wrote home to a friend:

At present we weavers are on strike: we are asking for an eight-hour day and a pay raise of 25% and I can tell you in all truth that, if we were in Italy, by this time Italian injustice would have already interfered, passing judicial condemnations. But here, as you well know, there is an extensive freedom to strike and freedom of speech, and now, although the struggle has already been going on for four weeks, we have reached a point where the bosses have almost accepted that our union is strong enough to win and to obtain that which their bullying behavior has taken away from us.

In 1886 the Federal Labor Commissioner issued a report that showed just where the worker stood. The average worker brought home a wage of $7.50 a week. But many didn't work year round. A textile mill hand who had to support a large family—with five or more children—might be given work only nine months a year and paid only $1.50 a day. Workers, said a witness before a Senate committee, "almost invariably live in filthy tenement houses or in cellars or garrets. . . . They are really uninhabitable. Swarms of children go about the street nearly naked; they are growing up to be the worst part of the community. They know no education."

Rents in the slums, where most urban immigrants lived, were $10 to $15 a month—a huge sum to be taken out of weekly earnings of $8 or less.

The cities that drew immigrants desiring work in their factories found room for them only in the overcrowded slums. Jacob Riis, a reporter (himself a Danish immigrant), with his pencil and camera pried into the darkest corners of the slums on New York's Lower East Side. He studied the system he called "the evil offspring of public neglect and private greed" and described it in his book, *How the Other Half Lives!*

It was the greed of the landlords that fostered the slum, said Riis:

They saw in the homeless crowds from over the sea only a chance

Homeless immigrants find shelter in a shed.

Boys scavenging for food in trash barrels

for business, and exploited them to the uttermost, making some-times a hundred percent on the capital invested—always most out of the worst houses, from the tenants of which nothing was expected save that they pay the usurious rents.

Many of those tenements were workshops as well as homes, soon tagged "sweatshops."

What New York's sweatshops did to a working family's life was reported by John DeWitt Warner in *Harper's Weekly* in 1895:

The contractors' shops are much like other factories—the large proportion of foreign labor and a tendency toward long hours being their main distinctions. In the tenement "sweatshops" unhealthy and unclean conditions are almost universal, and those of filth and contagion common. The employees are in the main foreign-born and newly arrived. The proportion of female labor is large, and child labor is largely used. Wages are from a fourth to a third less than in the larger shops. As to hours, there is no limit except the endurance of the employees, the work being paid for by the "task," and the task so adjusted as to drive from the shop any employee who, whenever he is given a bench, will not work to the limit of physical endurance, the hours of labor being rarely less than twelve, generally thirteen or fourteen, frequently from fifteen to eighteen hours in the twenty-four. The lot, however, of these "sweatshop" workers is a luxury compared to that of those engaged in tenement homework. The homeworker is generally a foreigner just arrived, and frequently a woman whose husband is dead, sick or worthless, and whose children keep her at home. Of these ten-ement homeworkers there are more women than men, and chil-dren are as numerous as both. The work is carried on in the one, two, or three rooms occupied by the family, with its subtenants or

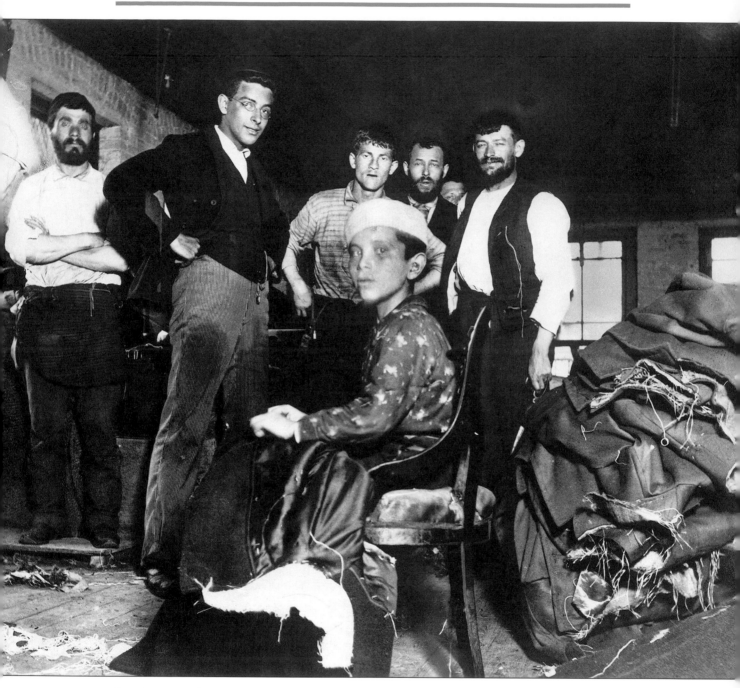

Immigrant workers in a New York sweatshop in the 1880s pause to face the photographer, Jacob Riis. The young boy in the foreground is among the thousands of child laborers deprived of schooling to help support their families.

boarders. No pretence is made of separating shop work from household affairs. The hours observed are those which endurance alone limits. Children are worked to death beside their parents. Contagious diseases are especially prevalent among these people; but even death disturbs from their occupation only the one or two necessary to dispose of the body.

As to wages in this "tenement homework," there is nothing which can properly be so called. The work is secured by underbidding of tenement sweatshops, and is generally piece-work, one process of which may be attended to by the head of the family, and the rest by its other members according to their capacity. Those engaged are so generally compelled to accept rather than to choose their work that it is taken without reference to the possibility of gaining a livelihood therefrom, the miserable workers earning what they can, begging to supplement it, and dying or being supported as paupers when they fail.

In Chicago, a citizens' committee investigated the tenement areas of that city in 1883–1884. Their report told of

The wretched conditions of the tenements into which thousands of workingmen are huddled, the wholesale violation of all rules for drainage, plumbing, light, ventilation and safety in case of fire or accident, the neglect of all laws of health, the horrible conditions of sewers and outhouses, the filthy, dingy rooms into which they are crowded, the unwholesome character of their food, and the equally filthy nature of the neighboring streets, alleys and backlots filled with decaying matter and stagnant pools.

It was much the same in any city you could name. Children of immigrants were fated to suffer the worst. Their death toll was the highest—

Homeless street kids

the outcome of bad sanitation, malnutrition, disease.

Millions of slum dwellers were immigrants. Because they were poor they had to live in the heart of the city or industrial community. They clung together to be close to the people whose customs and language they knew. Their colonies were often in the worst, most criminal, and politically corrupt parts of the city. Take Baltimore: 77 percent of the slum population was of foreign birth or parentage; in Chicago, it was 90 percent; in Philadelphia, 91 percent; in New York, 95 percent.

The slums, wrote Robert Hunter, author of a study in the early 1900s, became "wildernesses of neglect, almost unexplored and almost unknown" to the people on the upper end of society. It was a sorry school for the immigrant to learn what America was, and what it stood for. In 1890, of America's 12.5 million families, 11 million had an average income of $380 a year. The richest 1 percent of the country enjoyed wealth greater than the total of the remaining 99 percent.

As part of the Americanization process, immigrant children learn to salute the flag under the watchful eyes of their teacher.

Ten

Becoming
Americans

AS THE IMMIGRANTS POURED IN, THEY WERE URGED TO ASSIMILATE QUICK-ly. The goal of the public schools was to Americanize the newcomers. But in what way? The message was that if you wanted to make it here, you must become "real" Americans. Drop what made you different, forget where your parents came from and what they had brought with them—their language, their culture, their beliefs, their values.

Ole Rolvaag, the Norwegian author of *Giants in the Earth*, who was educated mostly in America, describes how this happened:

> Again and again [second-generation Norwegians] have had impressed on them: all that has grown on American earth is good, but all that can be called *foreign* is at best suspect. Many of our own people have jogged in the tracks of the jingoists. "Norwegian church service? Why should there be Norwegian church service in

America? No, talk English. . . . No full blooded American can be expected to want to belong to a Norwegian church!" . . . The young are extremely sensitive in matters of honor, and much more so in their patriotic honor! It has been—and to some extent still is—a point of honor to be able to prove that nothing *foreign* hangs about one's person. Under such conditions how could anyone expect that young people should show only enthusiasm for their forefathers' tongue—that would be to expect the impossible.

Immigrants were made to feel their languages and cultures were inferior and unwelcome. They became the victims of stereotypes in the popular media of that time—vaudeville, movies, theater, cartoons, advertising. The effect was to demolish the character of people from other countries. Stereotypes are used to justify prejudice. These were strongest toward people of color. But not only to them. Immigrants all, whether European, Hispanic, or Asian, were put down, distrusted, and feared.

Many of the dominant white Anglo-Saxon Protestants said the newcomers wouldn't fit into American life. Why, they might overturn the government in a bloody revolution!

But others said, no, don't worry; America is a melting pot of different peoples. Each ethnic group arriving on these shores will lose its identity and take on the cultural characteristics of white Anglo-Saxon Protestants. And this uniformity, this sameness, this conformity to one model, was greatly prized.

Some advanced thinkers had a different view of the melting pot theory. They saw immigrant culture not as something to be boiled away in a pot. Don't ask the immigrant to exchange the old culture for a new American one, they said. Rather, let's create a new identity that will contain the best elements of each. A mosaic, rather than a melting pot.

But the great majority of Americans, including many of the immigrants and their children, believed that abandoning their old ethnic culture

Grandmothers, too, are helped along the path to citizenship. Five elderly women, born in (from left to right) Hungary, Galicia, Russia, Germany, and Romania, join in making a huge American flag while their instructor looks on.

was the only way to become American. Under such pressure many immigrants changed names that typified the old country. Family as well as first names had to go. Russian, Germanic, Italian, Greek—were reshaped into English-sounding names. This was a defensive measure too, for many firms refused to hire people with "funny" names. For the immigrants who hungered to be "true" Americans, clothing had to be changed, English mastered. Many parents not only sent their kids to public school but went to night school themselves. Secular education was seen as the door to success in America.

The pressure for total and rapid assimilation often harmed relations between parents and children. As their ways diverged, children came to look down upon their parents' "foreign" accents, lifestyles, and beliefs.

The young often judged their parents harshly, upon the most superficial standard of Americanism: What's neat? Cool? With it?

In the early 1900s many articles and books began to voice fears about the most recent immigrants. They tried to prove that ethnic groups were unequal in natural intelligence, and that Jews, Italians, Slavs, and others were inferior peoples.

Even some liberal historians, sociologists, and economists of that period took up racist appeals. They held that democracy was superior because Anglo-Saxons were superior. Keep out these ignorant, filthy, coarse breeds pouring out of Ellis Island or America will degenerate, they cried.

Robert Hunter, the social reformer, in 1912 warned his readers that what he called the "evils" of immigration might be permanent, not temporary:

The direct descendants of the people who fought for and defended the Republic and who gave us a rich heritage of democratic institutions, are being replaced by the Slavic, Balkan, and Mediterranean peoples. . . . In the United States the peasantry from other countries, degraded by foreign oppression, are supplanting the

Melting Pot?

Louis Adamic, an immigrant from Yugoslavia, became a citizen while serving in the U.S. Army during World War I. In 1938, in his book *My America*, he had this to say about his adopted country:

> America is only beginning, and every beginning is somewhat of a mess. . . . America is chopped up into numerous racial, class, and cultural islands surrounded by vague seas, with scant connection and communication among them. The old Melting Pot or Crucible idea has not been carried out any too well. Human America is poorly integrated, and I am for integration and homogeneity, for the disappearance of the now sharply defined, islandlike groups, and the gradual organic merging of all into a nation that culturally and spiritually will be a fusion of all the races and nations now in the United States.

descendants of the original stock of this country. This is race suicide. Blacks much more than any other group were affected in that era, and suffered segregation, race riots, and lynchings. In the 1920s African Americans, Jews, and Catholics became the special targets of the revived Ku Klux Klan, a secret society founded in the South after the Civil War.

When the United States entered World War I the task of Americanizing the newcomers shifted from largely private groups to the government. Now only 100 percent Americans would do. Both federal and state governments demanded that immigrants demonstrate their absolute loyalty to the United States. No longer was there room for "divided loyalty." Anyone who spoke of retaining elements of foreign cultures, including native languages, was accused of being "un-American." The war hardened the belief that certain kinds of immigrants should be barred from entering America.

A loud and strong chorus began calling for laws to restrict immigration. In 1917 Congress passed a bill that limited immigration by means of a literacy test. In 1921 another law adopted a system of numerical restriction based upon nationality. Then, in 1924, the Johnson-Reed Act slammed the door on mass immigration. It set a ceiling of 150,000 immigrants a year, and adopted a quota formula that would remain in effect for forty-one years. It fixed the quota of each nation at 2 percent of the number of immigrants here in 1890. After 1929 a permanent ceiling of 150,000 persons a year was set, with quotas based on the 1920 census. Because more than two-thirds of Americans in 1920 were from Northern Europe, the goal was clear: to keep the Nordics on top. So everyone else who wanted to enter had to sit on long waiting lists. Their small quotas were always filled.

By 1965 court orders secured under the pressure of the civil rights movement had dismantled legal segregation; new federal laws banned discrimination in public housing, employment, and voting. There was no longer any legal basis for second-class citizenship. In that same year Congress adopted the Hart-Celler Act. It dropped the national origins quota system and substituted "family reunification" and job skills as the

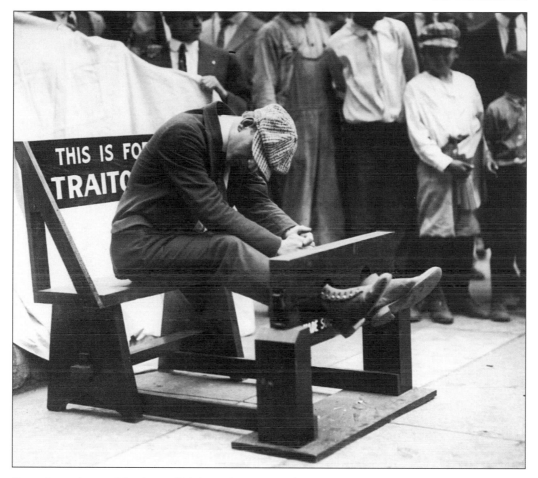

In stocks and on public view, officials made an example of this immigrant whose loyalty had been called into question.

new, nonracial criteria for immigration. The chief result of the new law was to open America's door to a flood of newcomers from Latin America, the Caribbean, and Asia.

Ten years later, in 1976, a public opinion poll showed that 85 percent of the respondents agreed with the statement: "The United States was meant to be . . . a country made up of many races, religions, and nationalities."

A family from Colombia poses proudly before their soon-to-be-completed home in the United States.

Eleven

Today: The New Immigrants

AMERICA IS NOW EXPERIENCING THE SECOND GREAT MIGRATION. THIS second wave began at the end of the 1960s, and is still going on. Remember that the First Great Migration, between 1880 and 1924, brought 26 million people to the United States. It changed the course of American social and economic history.

As the twenty-first century begins, at least 30 million persons have already migrated here in this second wave.

What the long-term effects of the current wave will be, no one knows. About the immigration of the past, however, who can doubt that America has been blessed by it? These immigrants developed our land, built our cities and industries, and enriched our culture.

Today a debate over immigration policy figures in the media almost every day. It is an issue that has caused heated debate throughout American history. How many immigrants should be admitted, if any?

And if some, which visa applicants from which countries? The costs and benefits are weighed, with people coming down on one side or another. At certain times in the past, as we've seen, the outcome has been to shut the door on more newcomers. At other times, the decision has been for an open-door policy.

The booming economy that began in the 1990s drained the pool of available workers. As the labor market got tight, immigrants flowed in from across the borders. Is it any wonder? When by United Nations estimates 3 billion people live on less than $2 a day? By the year 2000 it was estimated there were at least 6 million illegal immigrants in America. Although crossing the borders isn't easy, many enter without documents, or with forged documents, or by abusing documents such as a tourist's visa.

According to official data gathered in the year 2000, the foreign-born held about 12 percent of all jobs. In several American cities—Atlanta, Cincinnati, Louisville, Indianapolis—Hispanic immigrants held a large portion of construction jobs. In Lawrence, Massachusetts, most of the workers in a textile mill were Hispanic immigrants. In Chicago a third of the 1,500 laundry workers in a union local were undocumented workers.

Another way to see the influx of immigrants is to check their presence in large cities. Take New York: the Woodside neighborhood, in 2000, counted people from 49 different countries who spoke 34 different languages. Ten years before, Woodside's foreign-born population was 55 percent; in East Harlem, it was 36 percent; on the Lower East Side, 54 percent; in Bensonhurst, 40 percent.

Today these percentages are certainly larger. For the new arrivals come from more countries and speak more languages than the First Great Wave of European immigrants. They are more economically varied, with highly educated and skilled people among them. And more than those earlier newcomers, they tend to avoid ethnic ghettos, scattering throughout the cities.

Immigrant Children

P.S. 139, an elementary public school in Queens, New York, is typical of those communities where large numbers of immigrants have recently settled. The chart on this page tells what the primary home language of the students was in 2000. Among the 861 students, 36 different languages were spoken.

Melting Pot

PRIMARY HOME LANGUAGE OF STUDENTS ATTENDING PUBLIC SCHOOL 139 IN QUEENS.	NUMBER OF STUDENTS	PRIMARY HOME LANGUAGE OF STUDENTS ATTENDING PUBLIC SCHOOL 139 IN QUEENS.	NUMBER OF STUDENTS
Russian	200	Ukrainian	5
English	189	Bengali	4
Spanish	174	Polish	4
Mandarin	53	Portuguese	4
Cantonese	44	Georgian	3
Korean	40	Serbo-Croatian	3
Hindi	30	French	2
Chinese, other or unidentified dialects	21	Japanese	2
		Khoisan	2
Philipino	10	Czech	1
Hebrew	8	French-Khmer	1
Indonesian	8	Greek	1
Romanian	8	Hungarian	1
Urdu	8	Malayalam	1
Dari/Farsi/Persian	7	Sinhalese	1
Albanian	6	Slovenian	1
Arabic	6	Tamil	1
Bulgarian	6	Yornba	1
Gujarati	5	Source: P.S. 139 Queens	

TODAY: THE NEW IMMIGRANTS

Immigrants now make up a large part of the work force in dozens of industries. They work on farms, in hotels, construction, meat packing, and many other industries. They are increasingly valued by corporate America. Thousands of restaurants, hotels, farms, poultry plants, garment factories, and gardening companies would be forced to close for want of workers if immigrants were shut out or thrown out. The flow of immigrants affects not only the service economy. The high-tech sector insists the government should encourage the immigration of highly skilled people too.

Demographers predict that by 2005 Hispanics will become the nation's largest minority group, and by midcentury fully one-fourth of the total population. Although joined by a common language, they come from twenty-odd Latino countries with distinct histories, customs, and blends of European, African, and indigenous stock. They too, like all the other newcomers, come with hope of becoming integrated into the mainstream.

A five-year-old Laotian child cheers on his mother at her naturalization ceremony in Seattle.

A Note on Sources

The bibliography on migration to America from all parts of the world is vast. What follows is a selected list. It includes essays and books by historians, economists, sociologists, demographers, policymakers, and others. Some, written by members of a single ethnic group, describe personal experiences, perhaps in the form of memoirs. Others are scholarly studies of specific ethnic communities.

Historians are by no means all of one opinion on the causes and consequences of mass migration. Sometimes they change their views as continuing research produces new evidence. And scholars holding conflicting views don't hesitate to challenge one another in print.

Migration is a fascinating if complex story. Anyone who dips into it will surely find facets that reflect and illuminate his or her own family experience, whether of today, yesterday, or centuries ago.

Bibliography

Adamic, Louis. *My America 1928–1938*. New York: Harper, 1938.

Bailyn, Bernard. *The Peopling of British North America: An Introduction*. New York: Knopf, 1986.

Bielinberg, Andy, ed. *The Irish Diaspora*. London: Pearson, 2000.

Birmingham, Stephen. *America's Eastern European Jews*. Syracuse: Syracuse University Press, 2000.

Bodnar, John. *The Transplanted: A History of Immigrants in Urban America*. Bloomington: Indiana University Press, 1985.

Borjas, George J. *Heaven's Door: Immigration Policy and the American Economy*. Princeton: Princeton University Press, 1999.

Brown, Judith and Rosemary Foot, eds. *Migration: The Asian Experience*. New York: St. Martin's, 1994.

Burrow, Edwin G. and Mike Wallace. *Gotham: A History of New York City to 1898*. New York: Oxford, 1999.

Butwin, Frances. *The Jews in America: A History and Sources*. Minneapolis: Lerner Publications Co., 1969, rev. ed. 1991.

Chalian, Gérard and Jean-Pierre Rageau. *The Penguin Atlas of Diasporas*. New York: Viking, 1995.

Coffey, Michael, ed. *The Irish in America: A History*. Boston: Little Brown, 1997.

Daniels, Roger. *Coming to America: A History of Immigration and Ethnicity in American Life*. New York: Harper, 1990.

Daniels, Roger. *Not Like Us: Immigrants and Minorities in America, 1890–1924.* Chicago: Ivan Dee, 1997.

Flanders, Stephen A. *Atlas of American Migration.* New York: Facts on File, 1998.

Gabaccia, Donna. *From Sicily to Elizabeth Street.* Albany: State University of New York Press, 1984.

Glazer, Nathan and Daniel P. Moynihan, eds. *Ethnicity: Theory and Experience.* Cambridge: Harvard, 1975.

Glazer, Nathan, ed. *Clamor at the Gates: The New American Immigration.* New York: ICS, 1985.

Gonzalez, Juan. *Harvest of Empire: A History of Latinos in America.* New York: Viking, 2000.

Green, Nancy L., ed. *Jewish Workers in the Modern Diaspora.* Berkeley: California, 1998.

Handlin, Oscar. *The Uprooted.* Boston: Little Brown, 1951.

Hoerder, Dirk and Horst Rossler, eds. *Distant Magnets: Expectations and Realities in The Immigrant Experience, 1840–1930.* New York: Holmes & Meier, 1993.

Johnson, Daniel and Rex Campbell. *Black Migration in America.* Durham: Duke, 1981.

Jones, Maldwyn A. *American Immigration.* 2nd ed. Chicago: U. of Chicago, 1992.

Kaplan, Robert. *The Ends of the Earth.* New York: Random, 1996.

Kenny, Kevin. *The American Irish: A History.* London: Pearson, 2000.

King, Desmond. *Making Americans: Immigration, Race and the Origins of the Diverse Democracy.* Cambridge: Harvard, 2000.

Kwon, Peter. *Forbidden Workers: Illegal Chinese Immigrants and American Labor.* New York: New Press, 1998.

Landes, David S. *The Wealth and Poverty of Nations.* New York: Norton 1998.

LeMay Michael and Elliott R. Barham, eds. *U. S. Immigration and Naturalization Laws and Issues.* Westport: Greenwood, 1999.

Luebke, Frederick, ed. *European Immigrants in the American West.* Albuquerque: New Mexico, 1998.

Meltzer, Milton. *A History of Jewish Life from Eastern Europe to America.* Northvale, N.J.: Jason Aronson, 1996.

Mills, Nicolaus, ed. *Arguing Immigration: The Debate Over the Changing Face of America*. New York: Touchstone, 1994.

Nugent, Walter. *Crossings: The Great Transatlantic Migration, 1870–1914*. Bloomington: Indiana, 1995.

Perlmutter, Philip. *Legacy of Hate: A Short History of Ethnic, Religious and Racial Prejudice in America*. New York: Sharpe, 2000.

Rockaway, Robert A. *Words of the Uprooted*. Ithaca: Cornell, 1998.

Reimers, David M. *Still the Golden Door: The Third World Comes to America*. New York: Columbia, 1994.

Schoener, Allen, ed. *Portal to America: The Lower East Side, 1870–1925*. New York: Holt, 1976.

Sowell, Thomas. *Migration and Cultures: A World View*. New York: Basic, 1996.

Takaki, Ronald. *A Diffused Mirror: A History of Multicultural America*. Boston: Little Brown, 1993.

Thernstrom, Stephen. *Harvard Encyclopedia of American Ethnic Groups*. Cambridge: Belknap, 1980.

Ungar, Sanford J. *Fresh Blood: The New American Immigrants*. New York: Simon & Schuster, 1995.

Weimer, Myron. *The Global Migration Crisis: Challenge to States and to Human Rights*. New York: HarperCollins, 1995.

Further Reading

Bode, Janet. *The Color of Freedom: Immigrant Stories*. Danbury, CT: Watts, 1999.

———. *New Kids in Town: Oral Histories of Immigrant Teens*. New York: Scholastic, 1991.

Collier, Christopher, and James Lincoln Collier. *A Century of Immigration: 1820–1920*. Drama of American History series. New York: Marshall Cavendish, 1999.

Kurelek, William, and Margaret S. Engelhart. *They Sought a New World: The Story of European Immigration to North America*. Plattsburgh, NY: Tundra, 1985.

Lawlor, Veronica. *I Was Dreaming to Come to America: Memories from the Ellis Island Oral History Project*. New York: Penguin Putnam, 1997.

Reimers, David M. *A Land of Immigrants*. Immigrant Experience series. Broomall, PA: Chelsea House, 1995.

Roleff, Tamara L., ed. *Immigration*. San Diego: Greenhaven, 1998.

Index

Page numbers in **boldface** are illustrations and tables.